Y0-BPT-397

Cell Phones and Society

How Do Cell Phones Affect Health?

Other titles in the *Cell Phones and Society* series include:

How Do Cell Phones Affect Health?

Patricia D. Netzley

612
N

T 81618

'15

San Diego, CA

For more information, contact:
ReferencePoint Press, Inc.
PO Box 27779
San Diego, CA 92198
www.ReferencePointPress.com

LIBRARY OF CONGRESS CATALOGING-IN-PUBLICATION DATA

Netzley, Patricia D., author.
 How do cell phones affect health? / by Patricia D. Netzley.
    pages cm. — (Cell phones and society series)
 Audience: Grade 9 to 12.
 Includes bibliographical references and index.
 ISBN-13: 978-1-60152-670-0 (hardback)
 ISBN-10: 1-60152-670-9 (hardback)
 1. Cell phones—Health aspects—Juvenile literature. 2.—Low-level radiation—Health aspects—Juvenile literature. 3. Radio waves—Health aspects—Juvenile literature. I. Title.
  RA569.3.N48 2015
  612'.014481—dc 3
                                                                      2014003309

Contents

Do Cell Phones Pose Risks to Health and Well-Being?

Introduction

In June 2013 the *Northeast Times* newspaper asked high school students in Philadelphia, Pennsylvania, to talk about how important cell phones are in their daily lives. Several said they could not imagine life without a phone. "My daily routine is regulated by my cell phone," one student said. "I wake up because of the alarm of my cell phone. . . . Without my phone, my life would be a wreck." Another insisted, "I simply cannot live without my cell phone. . . . My cell phone is now my email device, camera, Twitter dashboard, social network controller and game console. In fact, I use my cell phone to research information rather than the computer. Without it I feel disconnected from the world."[1]

The number of people who feel this way is growing. Lee Rainie, director of the Pew Research Center's Internet & American Life Project, reports that Pew surveys indicate that people's reliance on cell phones has risen dramatically over the years. In fact, she says that "the cell phone is the most quickly adopted consumer technology in the history of the world."[2] Pew surveys in 2012 and 2013 found that 78 percent of Americans ages twelve to seventeen have their own cell phones, with 37 percent of them owning a smartphone. Ninety-one percent of adults in the United States own cell phones as well, and 63 percent of them use their phones to go online. In addition, Americans ages eighteen to twenty-nine send an average of eighty-eight text messages and make seventeen phone calls every day.

The rise in popularity of the cell phone is due to the many benefits that these devices provide. They make communication easy through talking or texting, and they allow people to summon help in an emergency. Advanced devices known as smartphones also provide con-

> "I simply cannot live without my cell phone."[1]
>
> —A high school student in Philadelphia, Pennsylvania.

nectivity to the Internet, enabling users to perform a variety of functions that they previously could do only with a computer. The allure of such devices has led Strategy Analytics, a company that tracks and predicts business trends related to technology, to predict that by the end of 2015 there will be 2 billion active smartphone users worldwide, double that of 2012.

Matters of Controversy

Most people understand the attraction of smartphones and other types of cell phones. But some believe that in addition to their many benefits, cell phones have the potential to harm their users physically and/or mentally. Among those expressing concerns over the spread of cell phone use is the World Health Organization (WHO). WHO believes that cell phones can cause cancer and other health problems.

A common sight at kitchen tables and restaurants today is a person checking a cell phone and sometimes also a laptop while eating a meal. Many people, young and old, feel the need to constantly check their electronic devices.

The organization also believes that electromagnetic interference from cell phones can cause dangerous equipment malfunctions. In addition, WHO notes that cell phones can cause fatal or near-fatal accidents when used while driving.

All of these concerns, however, are a matter of controversy to one degree or another. For example, in the case of cell phone use while driving, a behavior that is banned in many places, people disagree on which types of cell phone use are more dangerous. Whereas many think that using a hand-held phone while behind the wheel, whether to call or to text, poses the greatest risk of having an accident, some experts say that calling with a hands-free device is just as dangerous.

More passionate disagreements surround the issue of whether there is a link between cancer and cell phone use. Some people say this idea is nonsense because scientific research has not proved that such a link exists. Nonetheless, surveys have shown that roughly 30 percent of Americans believe otherwise. Moreover, because there are only fifteen years' worth of data on the effects of cell phone use on the human body, some experts note that the long-term consequences of excessive cell phone use might not yet be known. In fact, after interviewing researchers involved in a 2010 study that found no link between brain cancer and cell phone use, Daniel Cressey of the scientific journal *Nature* reported, "Even the researchers involved in the trial do not all agree on the meaning of their work, with some apparently urging a cautious approach and suggesting that people should limit their phone use."[3]

> "The idea of being present in the moment is disappearing faster than you can say, 'Hey, I've got to take this call.'"[4]
>
> —*Journalist Mark Glaser.*

Psychological and Social Problems

Other experts suggest that cell phone use should be limited because a dependence on phones can cause problems in the way a user relates to other people and to the environment. Mark Glaser, a journalist who writes about issues related to technology, explains: "The idea of being present in the moment is disappearing faster than you can say, 'Hey, I've got to take this call. . . .' We devalue our current situation, the friends and family around us, our surroundings and setting, for something going on somewhere else."[4]

Some experts have noted that cell phone users can become so dependent on their devices that they experience great distress when access to their phone is denied. Studies have also shown an apparent link between heavy cell phone use and both depression and sleep problems, especially among young people. Still, it is unlikely that warnings about the possible hazards of cell phone use will slow the speed at which people are adopting this technology, especially given that experts cannot agree on just how serious these hazards are.

Can Cell Phones Cause Cancer?

Chapter One

For twelve years Innocente Marcolini, a sixty-year-old business-man in Italy, used a cell phone for five to six hours every workday. Then he fell ill and was diagnosed as having a brain tumor in a location close to where he held his cell phone to his head while talking. A surgeon was able to remove this tumor, but afterward Marcolini was left with a partially paralyzed face. Unable to work, he applied to the Italian Workers' Compensation Authority, which provides financial aid to people injured on the job. Marcolini claimed that his tumor had been caused by his work—or more specifically, by the cell phone he used for his work.

Radiation Concerns

Marcolini's claim relied on the view held by some physicians that heavy cell phone use may lead to two types of rare brain cancers: glioma and acoustic neuroma. Those who support this view argue that cell phones are capable of causing changes in the brain because they emit signals via radio waves. Radio waves are made up of radio frequency (RF) energy, a type of electromagnetic radiation that is the reason for concerns about cancer.

Electromagnetic radiation comes in two types, ionizing and non-ionizing, with these classifications based on whether the radiation can cause changes in atoms. (*Ionizing* is defined as converting an atom into an ion via the removal of one or more of the atom's electrons.) X-rays and gamma rays produce ionizing radiation, which, in high amounts, is known to cause cancer. Radio waves and microwaves are nonionizing, and experts disagree on whether they also pose a cancer risk and, if so, to what degree.

Many studies have tried to determine whether electromagnetic fields (EMFs) cause cancer. Although some have suggested that a link between cancers and EMFs might exist, others have denied any link. Consequently, for more than twenty-five years people have been arguing over the results of such studies, and government bodies that set rules regarding EMF exposure have largely ignored the possibility that exposure might be harmful. As EMF researcher Ray Lowenthal, a professor at the University of Tasmania, notes, "The evidence of detrimental long-term health effects is far from conclusive and international guidelines for limiting exposure to EMF are based on possible short-term effects rather than longer-term disease risks such as cancer."[5]

Lowenthal's own studies into EMF-related health issues have found that children who live within 984 feet (300 m) of high-voltage power lines, a source of EMFs, up until they are five years old are five times more likely to develop cancer, particularly leukemia, lymphoma, or multiple myeloma. Children who live even briefly near power lines prior to the age of fifteen are three times more likely to develop cancer once they become adults. Moreover, for every year that a per-

A cell tower rises high over a city. Electromagnetic fields, or EMFs, produced by cell towers have been cited by some as a possible cause of cancer, but many researchers say radiation emitted by cell towers is insignificant.

son lived within 164 feet (50m) of a power line, that person's risk of contracting cancer rose by 7 percent.

However, experts who have studied this data and the findings from similar studies note that many other environmental factors could have caused these cancers. Something in the soil where the children played, for example, might have been to blame, or something in their diets or households. Therefore, Bruce Armstrong, a professor of public health at Sydney University, says, "I think we are in a position where we have to say that there is a possibility that exposure to electromagnetic fields increases the risk of some cancers, but I don't think we know yet whether powerlines actually cause cancer."[6]

Cell Phone Towers

Nonetheless, studies like Lowenthal's have led to media speculation that cell phone towers, which also produce EMFs, might also cause leukemia and other cancers. But there are significant differences in the way cell phone towers and power lines work. Cell phone towers have antennae that transmit signals back and forth between phones intermittently, whereas power lines constantly carry energy, and the power levels in cell phone towers are much lower than those in power lines.

In addition, the EMF produced by a cell phone tower is from RF waves, and as the American Cancer Society explains,

> RF waves have long wavelengths, which can only be concentrated to about an inch or two in size. This makes it unlikely that the energy from RF waves could be concentrated enough to affect individual cells in the body. . . . [And] even if RF waves were somehow able to affect cells in the body at higher doses, the level of RF waves present at ground level is very low—well below the recommended limits. Levels of energy from RF waves near cell phone towers are not significantly different from the background levels of RF radiation in urban areas from other sources, such as radio and television broadcast stations.[7]

Given these differences, few scientists believe it is possible for a cell phone tower to cause health problems. Therefore, there have

Smartphone Thumb

Although people disagree on whether cell phones cause cancer, there is no doubt that these devices cause other kinds of damage to the human body. Among the most frequently seen physical effects are overuse injuries to thumbs due to excessive keypad use. Such injuries are commonly called BlackBerry thumb, smartphone thumb, or texting thumb. Caused by repetitive stress on the thumb joint, such injuries also can affect the wrist and hand because of the way that muscles and tendons in the hand are attached to the thumb. Inflammation of the tendons can cause a great deal of pain and reduce the sufferer's ability to grip things. Experts say that these injuries are on the rise. According to a 2013 study in Great Britain, two out of five cell phone users suffered from thumb pain within the last five years, and more than half of them owned smartphones.

been far fewer studies on the possibility that these towers might cause cancer in humans than there have been on the possible cancer risks associated with power lines. The American Cancer Society, however, reports that only one study on people living near cell phone towers has suggested that this might increase the risk of contracting cancer, but the increase was extremely slight and might have been due to other factors.

As for laboratory studies, the American Cancer Society reports that

most of these studies have supported the idea that the RF waves given off by cell phones and towers don't have enough energy to damage DNA directly. [DNA is the material within every cell in the body that carries information about how the living organism will develop and function.] Some scientists have reported that the RF waves may produce other effects in human cells (in lab dishes) that might possibly help tumors grow. However, these studies have not been verified, and these effects weren't seen in a study that looked at the blood cells from people living near a cellular phone tower.[8]

Charges of Bias

Given such studies, the International Agency for Research on Cancer (IARC), a well-respected organization that assesses cancer risks, has not expressed any concerns about the safety of living or working near cell phone towers. In addition, the agency has expressed only minor concerns about cell phones. The IARC conducted its own study on whether cell phones pose health risks, and in 2010 it reported that there was no clear-cut evidence that cell phone use significantly increases the risk of someone getting cancer, including brain tumors. Known as the Interphone study, this research included data suggesting that heavy users of cell phones might have a slightly higher risk of getting a brain tumor, but the agency classified this risk as still being extremely small.

When the Italian Workers' Compensation Authority evaluated Marcolini's claim that his brain tumor was caused by his cell phone, it cited the Interphone study in denying him compensation. But Marcolini refused to accept this decision and filed a civil lawsuit against the agency. When this case was heard, the civil court noted that the Interphone study was funded in part by the cell phone industry and therefore could not be considered to be impartial. Consequently, in making its decision the court relied instead on an independent study conducted between 2005 and 2009 by Lennart Hardell, a professor of oncology and cancer epidemiology with the University of Örebro in Sweden.

Reported in 2012, this research showed that using a cell phone heavily for ten years or more increased the risk of developing a brain tumor by an average of 290 percent. Based on this information, as well as testimony from two prominent cancer specialists asserting that the electromagnetic radiation emitted by cell phones is capable of damaging brain cells and producing tumors, the court ruled in Marcolini's favor. In October 2012 this verdict was upheld by Italy's highest civil court, the Supreme Court of Cassation.

Adamant Opposition

Many experts expressed dismay over the Supreme Court's decision. The prevailing view among scientists both at the time of the ruling and now is that no evidence exists of a cause-and-effect relationship between the RF emissions produced by cell phones and brain tumors or any other form of cancer. Many also disagreed with the Italian courts' position that the Interphone study was biased, pointing out that researchers did not have contact with those funding their work.

One of the most vocal supporters of the Interphone researchers' work has been Michael Repacholi, who was an expert in EMFs and environmental health for WHO prior to his retirement from the organization in 2006. Repacholi rejects the theory that cell phones can cause tumors. Upon the 2013 publication of his book *Mobile Phones and Public Health—Myths and Reality,* he stated, "From all the high quality studies that have been published and the reviews of all the studies by international and national public health authorities, it can be safely concluded that it has not been established that mobile phone use causes or is associated with any health risks."[9]

> "Scientific studies from all over the world have failed to prove any adverse effects from use of mobile phones and towers."[10]
>
> —*Technology expert Ravi V.S. Prasad.*

The editor of Repacholi's book, technology expert Ravi V.S. Prasad, goes one step further. He believes that the research has not found a link between cell phone emissions and cancer because it is impossible for such emissions to cause any damage. He says, "Scientific studies from all over the world have failed to prove any adverse effects from use of mobile phones and towers. Their energy emissions are one-thousandth of the energy from sunlight, and so can't impact on health."[10]

Brain Changes

Other researchers, however, reject the notion that cell phones cannot possibly have an impact on health, citing studies in which exposure to phone emissions has produced changes in the brains of animals. In one Greek study reported in 2012, researchers found that when mice were exposed to radiation from cell phones, the proteins in areas of their brains associated with learning and memory were damaged. When pregnant rats were exposed to such radiation, the brains of their fetuses were similarly altered.

A study at the Yale School of Medicine, published in the March 15, 2012, issue of *Scientific Reports,* showed that such changes can affect not only brain development but also future behavior. Led by Hugh S. Taylor, chief of the Division of Reproductive Endocrinology and

Infertility, this study involved putting a cell phone with a call in progress (though with the phone muted and silenced) above the cage of certain pregnant mice. Meanwhile, a control group of pregnant mice had a cell phone atop their cage that did not have a call in progress. In reporting on this study, Karen N. Peart of *Yale News* explains that

> the team measured the brain electrical activity of adult mice that were exposed to radiation as fetuses, and conducted a battery of psychological and behavioral tests. They found that the mice that were exposed to radiation tended to be more hyperactive and had reduced memory capacity. Taylor attributed the behavioral changes to an effect during pregnancy on the development of neurons in the prefrontal cortex region of the brain.[11]

Taylor notes that the affected area of the brain is associated in humans with attention deficit/hyperactivity disorder (ADHD), which causes people to have problems paying attention and sitting still. Therefore, he says, "We have shown that behavioral problems in mice that resemble ADHD are caused by cell phone exposure in the womb. The rise in behavioral disorders in human children may be in part due to fetal cellular telephone irradiation exposure."[12]

"We have shown that behavioral problems in mice that resemble ADHD [attention deficit/hyperactivity disorder] are caused by cell phone exposure in the womb."[12]

—Hugh S. Taylor of the Yale School of Medicine.

Cooking Brains?

Similarly, a Russian study reported in 2011 studied 196 seven- to twelve-year-olds who used cell phones. Researchers found that over a period of four years, the children's memory abilities declined and they experienced increased fatigue. Given such studies, the American Academy of Pediatrics advises parents to avoid putting their cell phones too close to their young children. In addition, Belgium, Turkey, and France have banned the sale and advertising of phones to young children. But others say not nearly enough is being done to prevent young children from being exposed to cell phone radiation. For example,

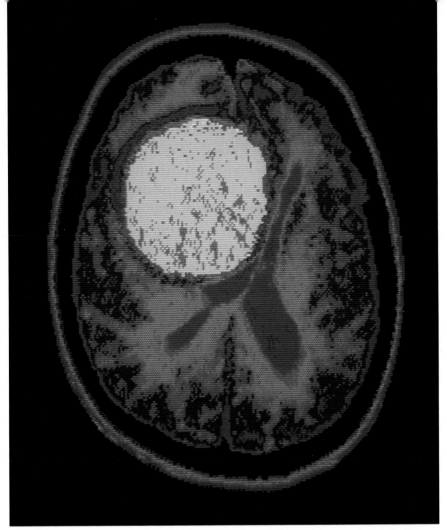

The large yellow mass visible in this colored brain scan is a tumor, or glioma. Some studies have found minimal risk of cell phone use causing such tumors, while others have come to the opposite conclusion.

the head of the Russian study, Professor Yury Grigoriev of the Russian National Committee on Non-Ionizing Radiation Protection, states that "the short-term and long-term potential consequences for society from exposing children to microwave radiation from cellular communication devices must be immediately acknowledged, globally, and responsibly addressed."[13]

Grigoriev refers to *microwaves* because both cell phones and microwave ovens use the same type of nonionizing radiation. Until recently most people believed that although microwave ovens produce heat, cell phones do not. Recent research suggests otherwise.

This has led Markham Heid of *Men's Health* magazine to warn, "Cell phone radiation may be slowly sautéing your noodle."[14]

Indeed, a study by radiation physicist David Gultekin of the Memorial Sloan-Kettering Cancer Center in New York, reported in the December 2012 issue of the *Proceedings of the National Academy of Sciences*, found that just a few minutes of exposure to cell phone emissions produce hotspots in the living brains of cows. These spots are so small that many experts doubt they pose health risks, although subjecting the brain to significant heat can damage the nervous system, cause hearing loss, and/or increase the risk of cancer. However, the results surprised those who assumed that because cell phones do not feel hot, they do not produce heat.

Activating the Brain

Nonetheless, the prevailing scientific view is that cell phones do not cause harm. As Nora Volkow, director of the National Institute on Drug Abuse at the National Institutes of Health, explains,

> right now someone that is in the manufacturing company could come to you and say prove to me that there's any harmful effects of cell phones. The cell phone technology has exploded, and there's really no clear-cut evidence of any harmful effects. And if there were harmful effects, because there are so many people exposed to it, it would have already become evident.[15]

Volkow was involved in a study that showed that after fifty minutes of constant use, cell phones affect the glucose metabolism of the brain in the area near the phone antenna. In explaining why she measured glucose metabolism—the conversion of blood sugar into energy—she says it was

> to try to answer that question: Is the human brain sensitive or not to the weak electromagnetic radiation that is delivered from cell phones when you place them by the side of your ear? And we use positron emission tomography to measure brain glucose metabolism, which serves as an indicator of brain function because when the brain is activated, glucose metabolism goes up.[16]

However, Volkow says it is unclear what this means. She admits, "We do not know what is the mechanism that is leading to the increase in glucose consumption, glucose metabolism. We interpret it to mean that the brain is activated because that's what happens when cells are activated: They increase the consumption of glucose. But how is that brought about?"[17]

According to Volkow, one theory is that cell phones increase brain temperature—something she calls a matter of controversy—and that this increase in temperature affects the amount of energy the brain needs. Another theory is that cell phones somehow excite the cells, making them require more energy. However, these and other theories do not address whether the brain's need for more energy is something harmful. As Volkow notes, "Activation of the brain in and of itself is not something negative. It's physiological. I am activating several areas of my brain [right now]. You want me to activate them because otherwise I wouldn't be functioning properly."[18] She adds, though, that the stimulation provided by a cell phone is not natural, and scientists do not know whether unnatural forms of stimulation have negative effects. Therefore, while her work shows that the brain is sensitive to cell phone emissions, it does not show that cell phones cause health problems.

> "Cell phone radiation may be slowly sautéing your noodle."[14]
>
> —*Markham Heid of* Men's Health *magazine.*

Volkow points out that her research also did not address the issue of whether exposure to electromagnetic radiation has long-term consequences. It also did not measure how long it takes brain glucose metabolism to go back to its normal state after cell phone use has stopped. Nor have there been studies on whether there are long-lasting changes to the brain because of the repeated stimulation caused by cell phone use. Perhaps, she says, this provides some unknown benefits to the brain. However, Volkow says that because so much is unknown, and because cell phones have not been in existence long enough to be certain that they will not cause problems after a lifetime of use, she uses a speakerphone or an earpiece attached to her cell phone rather than holding the device up to her head.

Keeping One's Distance

In fact, even cell phone manufacturers, who do not believe their devices are capable of causing harm, say that it is unwise to press a cell phone against the head—or other parts of the body. The cell phone manuals provided by some companies, including Apple and Motorola, advise that these devices be kept at least 0.4 inches (10 mm) away from the body at all times. (This is roughly the width of a pencil.)

Devra Davis, a leading American expert in environmental health, stresses the importance of following this instruction. She not only recommends that speakerphones be used whenever possible, but she also argues that it is unwise to store a cell phone close to the body while it is turned on. "Distance is your friend,"[19] she says. She adds that if a phone must be kept in a pocket, its back should be turned away from the body because a phone's EMF is transmitted through its back.

Cardiothoracic surgeon and television personality Dr. Oz (Mehmet Cengiz Öz) agrees that it is important to keep cell phones at a distance. On a December 6, 2013, episode of his popular television show on medical issues, he stated that he believes there is a definite link between cancer and cell phones. This episode included a segment featuring twenty-three-year-old Tiffany Frantz of Pennsylvania, who was diagnosed with breast cancer four years after she began carrying her cell phone in her bra next to her left breast every day from morning to night. The cancer developed in her left breast in an area that was in direct contact with the cell phone.

Otherwise healthy, Frantz immediately suspected that the cell phone was to blame, especially because she had no history of breast cancer in her family. Nonetheless, her doctors suspected that she had a genetic predisposition for the disease, especially given that breast cancer is rare in women under thirty and those who do contract the disease typically have a family history of it. However, genetic testing showed that the doctors' suspicion was wrong. Consequently, although they are unwilling to say they are absolutely sure Frantz's cell phone caused her disease, they are concerned about the possibility that such a link might exist. Frantz's local oncologist, Randall Oyer, says, "I never really thought about [the possibility of a link] until I met Tiffany. [Now] I take it very seriously. I'm very concerned about it. For now, the message needs to be: Don't put your cellphone in your

Infertility

Several studies have provided evidence that there might be a link between cell phone use and male infertility. Studies in 2007 and 2009, for example, found that subjecting rats to cell phone radiation can damage sperm. More recently, a 2011 study examined fifteen years' worth of health records at a fertility clinic, beginning in1993. The study found that the sperm of men who regularly used cell phones were 10 percent more likely to be damaged than the sperm of men who did not use cell phones (with 68 percent of cell phone users' sperm damaged versus 53 percent of nonusers). In another study, men who used a cell phone more than four hours a day had a far lower sperm count than men who used their phones less often. Still another study found that male sperm subjected to cell phone radiation over a distance approximating the space between a man's pants pocket and his genitals were significantly more damaged than when the distance was greater. This finding has led experts to suggest that men who are concerned about their fertility avoid storing their phone in a pants pocket, at least when the phone is on.

bra. Don't put it close to your body. And let's get the scientific research to answer the question, one way or another."[20]

Frantz agrees with this advice. She continues to suffer from her disease, which has spread to her hip, spine, pelvic bones, ribs, and skull despite the removal of her breast and radiation treatment. She therefore has had to repeat radiation treatments and currently takes cancer drugs and receives intravenous treatments to strengthen her bones. *The Dr. Oz Show* featured three other young women with similar problems who had also been carrying their cell phones in their bras for a long period. Each got cancer in the area of the breast where the phone had been resting.

Take Precautions

Given this anecdotal evidence as well as various studies that raise the possibility of a cell phone–cancer link, some experts argue that people should try to reduce the amount of time they carry an activated cell phone, especially since no one yet knows what effect several decades of exposure to cell phone radiation might have on the human body. Davis also recommends that calls not be made where signals are weak because a cell phone releases more radiation when it is struggling to search for and maintain a signal. For the same reason, radiation is strongest before the call is connected, so Davis suggests waiting to put the phone to the head (if the speaker phone feature cannot be used) until the person on the other end of the call has answered the phone. She and others note that it is unlikely that people will stop relying on cell phones for their communication needs, but they say that unless scientists are able to prove that cell phones cannot cause cancer, it is wise to take precautions to limit exposure to the devices' electromagnetic radiation.

The Hazards of Distraction

Chapter Two

In March 2013 nineteen-year-old Elizabeth Haley Meyers attempted to drive across a road in Gambrills, Maryland, while using her cell phone. She was so distracted by the device that she did not see an approaching motorcycle. Consequently, she drove into its path, causing motorcyclist Jonathan Wesley Roberts to run into the driver's side of her car. The crash caused him serious injuries, and he subsequently died at a hospital.

Shortly after the accident, Anne Colt Leitess of the State's Attorney's Office told reporters, "We have an eyewitness who was walking in the area. He saw her [Meyers] driving with one hand on the wheel and the other hand looking down and texting."[21] Later Meyers's cell phone records verified that this was the case. In October 2013 she was charged with negligent manslaughter by motor vehicle, criminal negligent manslaughter, reckless driving, negligent driving, failure to yield the right of way, and text messaging while driving. Texting while driving only became illegal in Maryland a few days before Meyers was charged with this crime, and if found guilty of committing manslaughter while texting, she will face ten years in prison.

Putting Everyone at Risk

Meyers's actions put everyone in the path of her vehicle at risk. She was also risking her own life because many drivers have been killed while attempting to use a cell phone. One of the most publicized examples is the January 2012 case of Taylor Sauer, an eighteen-year-old college student who was using her smartphone while making a four-hour late-night drive from Utah State University to her parents' home in Caldwell, Idaho. Sauer was sending a friend a message on Facebook about football when she accidentally ran into the back of a tanker truck. Police later said that Sauer was traveling at 80 miles per hour (129 km/h), and the truck was only going 15 miles per hour (24 km/h) up a hill.

Investigators later determined that Sauer had been posting messages on Facebook every ninety seconds during much of her drive. They also found no signs that she slammed on her brakes before hitting the truck, suggesting that she never saw it. At the time of the accident, texting while driving was not illegal in Idaho, although the state had a law against inattentive driving. Consequently, Sauer's parents called for a ban on texting while driving, not just in Idaho but also throughout the United States. They argued their case during television interviews and in front of their state legislature. While speaking about his daughter in one interview, Sauer's father said, "I think she was probably [texting] to stay awake, she was probably tired. But that's not a reason to do it, and the kids think they're invincible. To them, [texting] is not distracting, they're so proficient at texting, that they don't feel it's distracted driving."[22]

A Lack of Control

According to the US Centers for Disease Control and Prevention (CDC) in 2013, each day more than fifteen people are killed and more than twelve hundred are injured in crashes that have been reported to involve a distracted driver. Both the National Highway Traffic Safety Administration and the AAA cite cell phone use as the number one cause of driver distraction. In fact, according to the National Safety Council in 2011, at least 23 percent of all traffic accidents—or at least 1.3 million—involved cell phone use. Other studies have found that cell phone users between the ages of sixteen and nineteen are responsible for more than 20 percent of fatal car crashes in the United States.

Many phone-related accidents are the result of someone being too focused on the phone's keypad to drive safely. As an example of such an accident, in March 2012 sixteen-year-old Brianna McEwan of Norwalk, Connecticut, was using the keypad of her handheld smartphone to check her high school's webpage when she veered out of her lane and struck a man who had been jogging along the side of the road. He later died of his injuries, and McEwan was charged with negligent homicide. (She was found guilty but was given a suspended prison sentence as a youthful first-time offender.)

Another example of a death caused by paying too much attention to a keypad was the October 2012 case of nineteen-year-old Jona-

A driver checks messages on her phone while at the wheel. Texting while driving has become a major public health hazard.

thon Phillips of Holton, Indiana. Phillips was driving down a street at a speed of 38 miles per hour (61 km/h) while texting when he felt his car go over a bump. He thought he had run over an animal, so he stopped his car and got out to check. Phillips discovered that he had hit and killed a fourteen-month-old child who had run into the road.

Worse than Drunk Driving?

Current studies suggest that texting while driving is more dangerous than talking on a handheld phone while driving. In fact, in 2013 researchers at Cohen Children's Medical Center in New York reported that based on their evaluation of the circumstances surrounding teen deaths nationwide, texting while driving has become the leading cause of death for teen drivers. The head of the study, Andrew Adesman, says that he believes texting while driving has surpassed drunk driving as a cause of teen deaths because of how often teens are able to perform the activity. He explains, "We have very strong taboos against drinking and driving. Kids don't drink and drive every day. But some kids are out there texting and driving seven days a week—and they admit it."[23] Adesman reports that 50 percent of drivers in high school say they have texted while driving.

Studies that rely on observations of drivers support the prevalence of texting while driving. In one such study in 2013, researchers at the University of Washington used randomized observations at controlled intersections in various counties in Washington State to record driver behaviors. Many were engaged in distracting activities, but using a cell phone was by far the most common of these, even though texting or holding a cell phone to the ear while driving is illegal in the state. More than 8 percent of seventy-eight hundred drivers observed at these intersections were using an electronic device. Most of the devices were cell phones, and of the people using a cell phone, 45 percent were texting. Researcher Beth Ebel says of these results, "Personally, when I watch the behavior of someone who's texting and driving at the same time, it's chilling. I fear for that person. And I feel angry on behalf of the other folks on the road. We all deserve better."[24]

> "Kids don't drink and drive every day. But some kids are out there texting and driving seven days a week."[23]
>
> —Andrew Adesman of the Cohen Children's Medical Center in New York.

According to Ebel, studies have shown that texting while driving increases the risk of crashing a car by twenty-three times. She adds that this rate is similar to someone driving with a blood-alcohol level of 0.19, which is more than twice the limit of 0.08 that most states consider too drunk to drive. "For me texting and talking on the phone while you're driving is impaired driving," says Ebel. "It is no longer acceptable for people to drink while they drive or to drive after drinking. I'd like to see us make the same progress [with distracted driving]."[25]

Adverse Effects on Reaction Time

Other studies have also shown that texting adversely affects a driver's reaction time to a serious degree. One of the most significant of these studies was conducted by the Texas A&M Transportation Institute in October 2011. Also the first published study on the subject to be done under real driving conditions as opposed to a laboratory simula-

Train Accidents

It is dangerous to operate any kind of machinery or vehicle while using a cell phone—even a train, despite the fact that it is on a track. According to the Federal Railroad Association, between 2000 and 2008 there were 100 injuries and 30 fatalities in the United States caused by train operators being distracted by a cell phone or other electronic device. In 2008 a cell phone so distracted the operator of a commuter train in Chatsworth, California, that he collided head-on with a freight train, killing 25 people and injuring 135. Specifically, the operator of the commuter train was so busy texting to a friend that he ran through a red light and entered a single section of track already occupied by the oncoming freight train. More recently, in 2013 a high-speed train traveling from Madrid to Ferrol in northwest Spain derailed just outside the railway station at Santiago de Compostela, Spain, after taking a curve at up to 121 miles per hour (195 km/h) despite a 50 mile per hour (80 km/h) speed limit. In this case 79 people were killed and approximately 140 were injured. Investigators say that the train operator was talking on his cell phone and possibly also consulting a map at the time of the accident. Spain subsequently decided to prohibit train drivers from using mobile phones except in an emergency. After the Chatsworth crash, California's Public Utilities Commission instituted a similar ban.

tor, it required forty-two drivers ages sixteen to fifty-four to navigate a roughly 11-mile (18 km) test track that included a section lined with construction barrels. First the drivers completed the course without distractions, and then they drove the same track while sending and receiving text messages. During both trials they were supposed to stop whenever they spotted a flashing yellow light on the track, and the researchers measured how quickly they responded to this signal.

By the end of the test, researchers had discovered that texting added three to four seconds to the reaction time of drivers—if they managed to stop at all. While either reading or sending a text, a driver was eleven times more likely to drive right past the light, often not even noticing it. The head of the study, Christine Yager, concludes, "Essentially texting while driving doubles a driver's reaction time. That makes a driver less able to respond to sudden roadway dangers."[26] In addition, texting drivers had much more trouble maintaining a constant speed and staying in their driving lane.

Researchers also noted that other than the construction barrels, the course contained no driving hazards. In fact, it did not even contain any hills; drivers only had to go in a straight line, and there was no other traffic. Therefore, the researchers found the results of the study even more worrisome: "It is frightening to think of how much more poorly our participants may have performed if the driving conditions were more consistent with routine driving."[27]

Another study on reaction time, this one conducted by *Car and Driver* magazine, examined how far a car traveled after a texting driver responded to a red light. Researchers found that when a driver is reading a text or an e-mail on a phone, it adds roughly 36 feet (11 m) to the car's stopping distance; when the driver is sending a text, it

A high school senior demonstrates the difficulty of safely negotiating turns on an obstacle course while texting. When researchers put drivers through a similar course they found that texting drivers represent a major road hazard.

adds 70 feet (21 m). In contrast, a car being driven by someone who is legally drunk will take an average of just 4 feet (1 m) longer than normal to come to a stop. As with the Texas A&M study, researchers used a test track that did not challenge the drivers as much as real road conditions would. For instance, there were no pedestrians, no traffic signals, and no traffic. In more difficult circumstances, as Michael Austin of *Car and Driver* explains, one driver's habit of texting while "holding the phone up above the dashboard and typing with one hand would make it difficult to do anything except hit the brakes. And if anything in the periphery required a response, well, both drivers would probably be [in serious trouble].[28]

> "There are countless stories of teens dying in accidents because the driver was texting while driving."[29]
>
> —*Phil LeBeau of CBS News.*

Yet despite such results, the public still does not consider the issue of cell phone use behind the wheel to be a serious concern. As Phil LeBeau of CBS News said while reporting on this study,

The American public correctly views drinking and driving as wrong. But when it comes to texting and driving, we are not as outraged. Probably because many of us have done it and still do it . . . [even where it is banned]. Sadly, it will likely take more accidents and more deaths to change that attitude. There are countless stories of teens dying in accidents because the driver was texting while driving.[29]

Bans on Phones

To address this problem, an increasing number of states have banned the use of handheld phones by drivers. According to the National Conference of State Legislatures in January 2014, citing statistics from the Governor's Highway Safety Administration, at least twelve states ban the use of handheld cell phones while driving, and forty-one ban text messaging. Thirty-seven states ban all cell phone use for novice or teen drivers. In California, all drivers are banned from using a handheld cell phone while driving.

Texting While Walking

Most people know that texting while driving can be dangerous. Few consider that texting while walking can be dangerous as well. When walkers are too focused on their phones, they can trip over unseen objects, fall into ditches, stumble off curbs, run into posts or trees, or step in front of moving cars. Some of these accidents are deadly. Others result in a trip to the emergency room. Common distracted walking injuries include broken feet, ankles, legs, wrists, hands, and arms as well as facial fractures, nasal fractures, and blunt head trauma. A nationwide study conducted by Ohio State University revealed that in 2010 more than fifteen hundred pedestrians were treated for serious injuries caused by walking and using a cell phone at the same time, a number more than double that of 2005. Researchers believe this is only a fraction of the cases that actually occurred because many people are too embarrassed to admit that their injury was caused by such carelessness. Another study has shown that people also think they are far more competent at texting while walking than they really are. Conducted at Stony Brook University in New York in 2011, this study showed that twenty-year-olds were incapable of walking a straight line while texting, even though they subsequently told researchers that they thought they had done an excellent job on the walking test.

According to a University of California, Berkeley, study released in 2012, in the first four years since the California ban was enacted in July 2008, the number of deaths in the state that could be directly tied to the use of handheld cell phones was down 47 percent. Specifically, the number of deaths dropped from 100 to 53, and the number of injuries dropped from 7,720 to 3,862. In commenting on these findings at the time of their release, California senator Doug LaMalfa said they were no surprise. "When you ban something you're going to have less of it," he stated. "Of course the numbers are going to go down."[30]

But according to surveys taken nationwide, this is not necessarily the case. A federal survey of drivers age sixteen and older, released by the Department of Transportation in April 2013, shows that at any given time 660,000 drivers are looking at their cell phones when they should be looking at the road. A study released in March 2013 by the CDC found that nearly 70 percent of US drivers ages eighteen to sixty-four admitted that they talked on their phones while behind the wheel, as compared to 21 percent in the United Kingdom. Given these and other studies, the National Highway Traffic Safety Administration has said that there has been no significant reduction nationwide in cell phone use while driving, despite bans on the behavior.

Some experts believe the reason for this is that drivers do not believe they will get caught when they break the law—and indeed, this risk is low. As Jeff Larson of the Safe Roads Alliance in Boston, Massachusetts, notes, "Police are finding the laws on distracted driving difficult to enforce."[31] From outside of the car, it is not easy to tell when the driver is using a cell phone, especially for texting.

Connecticut high school student Brianna McEwan, who killed a jogger while using her smartphone to check a webpage, is a prime example of someone who broke a well-known state ban on using a handheld cell phone while driving. But as the victim's girlfriend, Dawn Jeffrey, pointed out at a February 2013 hearing to consider toughening distracted driving laws in Connecticut, McEwan had a lot of company in ignoring the law. Jeffrey said, "I dare any one of you to drive for more than five minutes without seeing someone with a phone behind the wheel of a car."[32]

> "I dare any one of you to drive for more than five minutes without seeing someone with a phone behind the wheel of a car."[32]
>
> —Dawn Jeffrey, the girlfriend of a man who was killed by a texting driver.

Hands-Free Distractions

Some people believe that cell phones will no longer pose driving dangers once all cars come equipped with hands-free phones. But studies suggest that hands-free phones are no safer to use while driving than handheld ones. One such study was led by psychologist David L. Strayer of the University of Utah, director of the Center for the Prevention of Distracted Driving. That 2011 study of college students' ability to drive while distracted, found that the driving performance of more than 97 percent of the students fell 20 to 30 percent when they tried to talk on a cell phone while operating a driving simulator. In other studies conducted using regular vehicles, Strayer found that even when road signs are pointed out to a driver talking on a hands-free cell phone, the driver quickly forgets having seen the signs. Strayer says that "cell-phone conversations made drivers more likely to miss traffic signals and react more slowly to the signals that they did detect," and "when a driver becomes involved in a cell-phone conversation, attention is withdrawn from the driving environment necessary for the safe operation of the vehicle."[33]

A highway sign warns drivers in Pennsylvania to abide by a 2012 law that bans texting while driving. Many states have gone further, banning any use of handheld cell phones while driving.

Experts say this is because cell phones engage the mind more fully than many other types of distractions. Whereas listening to the radio, for example, is a passive mental activity, both texting and talking are active mental activities because they require the mind to come up with things to say. This is borne out by studies showing that the act of trying to remember things associated with a phone conversation can diminish driving performance. One such study showed that it was hard for drivers to stay in their traffic lane while they were struggling to recall a phone number. Another study found that memorizing and reciting a list of words dictated during a call could diminish a driver's steering ability and braking time. The longer the list, the more trouble the driver had keeping the car in its lane.

Hands-free texting provides the same sort of distractions, and studies are beginning to show that this relatively new technology does not eliminate the dangers of texting while driving. In one study released in April 2013, conducted by the Texas A&M Transportation Institute, researchers found that although manual texting required a little less time to perform than the voice-to-text method, drivers had roughly the same problems to the same degree with their driving performance. The forty-three test subjects first navigated a driving course without using a cell phone so that their undistracted driving performance could be compared to their performance while distracted. Each driver then drove the course three times: once using the iPhone voice-to-text application, once using the comparable Android application, and once texting manually in order to perform a series of texting tasks. Researchers recorded how long it took for each driver to complete these tasks and how long it took for each driver to brake and stop their car at various times in response to a light that flashed at random intervals.

The researchers found that drivers took roughly twice as long to react to this light while texting no matter which texting method was used. Drivers also kept their eyes off the road to roughly the same degree regardless of the texting method used—a dangerous amount, the researchers said. Ironically, the participants felt that they were driving more safely while using the voice-to-text applications as compared to when they were texting manually, even though by objective measurements their driving performance was roughly the same—and just as substandard—for all types of texting.

The Risks of a Crash

Another texting study, conducted by the Virginia Tech Transportation Institute and reported in the January 2, 2014 issue of the *New England Journal of Medicine*, observed the behaviors of two groups of drivers. The first comprised 109 adults up to seventy-two years in age with an average of twenty years' experience behind the wheel. The second comprised forty-two teenagers who had had their driver's licenses for less than three weeks at the beginning of the study. The more experienced drivers were observed for a year and the younger ones for eighteen months.

Researchers placed a minimum of four video cameras in each driver's car, along with global positioning systems, lane trackers, devices to measure speed and acceleration, and other sensors that collected driving performance data. Drivers were told to drive as they normally would. Every time one of them had a crash or near crash (defined as a driving incident that required the driver to make any sort of maneuver to avoid a crash), the researchers noted whether the driver was engaged in a distracting behavior unrelated to their driving at the time.

Researchers found that for the novice drivers, reaching for a cell phone or dialing the phone increased the risk of crashing or nearly crashing by a factor of about 8, and sending or receiving a text message increased the risk roughly by a factor of 4. So few of the experienced drivers texted that the researchers could not assess this type of risk for the group, but dialing the phone increased the risk of such a driver having an accident or a near miss by a factor of approximately 2.5. The researchers also found that by the end of the study, most of the novice drivers had doubled the amount of time they spent using their cell phones, indicating that with driving confidence came more risky behavior.

More Research Is Needed

Experts say this finding is not surprising. However, many have expressed surprise and skepticism regarding another of the study's conclusions: that talking on a cell phone did not increase crash risk for either the novice or the experienced drivers. Strayer says that given his own studies, this conclusion has to be inaccurate and is probably caused by near misses not being recorded in the absence of erratic driving. As he explains, "You don't swerve so much when you're talking on a cellphone; you just might run through a red light,"[34] and this fact might be missed unless it resulted in a crash.

Many experts say this and other issues related to distracted driving require more research. In fact, Christine Yager, who managed the Texas A&M Transportation Institute study on voice-to-text apps, says, "Understanding the distracted driving issue is an evolving process." She adds, "We're eager to see what other studies may find."[35] Yet one thing is clear from existing studies and accident reports: using a cell phone while driving can result in someone's death.

Threats to Social and Psychological Well-Being

On January 13, 2014, seventy-one-year-old retired police officer Curtis Reeves was watching movie previews in a Florida theater with his wife when he became annoyed because the man sitting in front of him, forty-three-year-old former US Navy petty officer Chad Oulson, was texting. Reeves asked him to stop; Oulson ignored the request, intent on exchanging messages with his three-year-old daughter via the person caring for her while he and his wife were at the movies. Reeves left his seat to complain about the texting to the theater manager, but the manager was busy with another customer. Frustrated, Reeves returned to his seat to again confront Oulson.

The two men began to argue, and police later determined that during this altercation Oulson threw a bag of popcorn at Reeves. Reeves then pulled a semi-automatic handgun from his pants pocket, pointed it at Oulson's chest, and fired. Oulson later died at a hospital. Oulson's wife was also injured, having held out her hands in an attempt to shield her husband right before the fatal shot was fired.

After Reeves was arrested for the crime, a woman came forward to report that only three weeks earlier, in the same theater, Reeves had berated her for texting as well. Two other people said that Reeves had reported them for texting in the theater just two weeks earlier and had told another man to turn off his cell phone after it went off. These witnesses said that Reeves seemed more interested in monitoring cell phone use among theatergoers than in watching the movie.

Cell Phone Rage

In the aftermath of the shooting many people expressed sympathy for the victim and outrage over the fact that texting led to a death. However, some also understood Reeves's frustration. Surveys of college students have shown that 97 percent believe it is rude to use a cell phone in a theater (even though one-fourth of respondents admit to having done so themselves). Consequently, people understood Reeves's anger at having someone ruin his movie experience with the sounds and screen lighting associated with texting. Online columnist Jeffrey Wells suggests that the incident was partly Oulson's fault because of the ire that cell phone use in a theater is likely to trigger, saying that Oulson's "unconscionably selfish" behavior made Reeves so angry that he "couldn't hold it together." Wells adds that Oulson "obviously didn't deserve to die for texting, but you can't say he didn't at least flirt with the possibility of trouble by doing so."[36]

Indeed, extreme anger due to inconsiderate cell phone use has been a problem for years. As early as 2000, doctors at a Toronto hospital reported having treated people for black eyes and cracked ribs due to fights over cell phone conversations conducted in public places to the annoyance of everyone in earshot. The doctors dubbed the cause of these injuries "cell phone rage."[37] Over a decade later, people are still struggling to control their cell phone rage. For example, after listening to a Boston, Massachusetts, college student carry on a loud cell phone conversation about his personal problems for at least an hour during a bus ride, blogger Joan Johnson-Freese wrote, "The restraint I showed in not ripping the cell phone out of the hand of the young man two rows in front of me and crushing it under my heel was quite remarkable. But it was close." She also confessed, "My new hero is a guy in Russia who recently got out of his car and SMASHED the cell phone of another driver who almost caused an accident . . . because, not surprisingly he was talking on his phone. The video is priceless. Just watching it releases the same kind of tension as an hour of kickboxing."[38]

An Integral Part of Daily Life

People who use cell phones inconsiderately often do not realize how their behavior is affecting others because it has become such a habit that they reach for their phone without thinking. As Nancy Gibbs of *Time* magazine notes, smartphones and their access to the Internet have made people "accustomed to having all knowledge at our fingertips," and to many it would be unthinkable to leave their phone at home. She reports,

In the U.S., close to 9 in 10 adults carry a mobile, leaving its marks on body, mind, spirit. There's a smart-phone gait: the slow sidewalk weave that comes from being lost in conversation rather than looking where you're going. Thumbs are stronger, attention shorter, temptation everywhere: we can always be, mentally, digitally, someplace other than where we are.[39]

Psychiatrist David Greenfield, an expert on technology-related psychological issues, also notes that cell phones have made it difficult for people to cope with simply sitting and doing nothing. He explains, "People have no tolerance for boredom. They can't tolerate not doing something, because they have the world in their pockets [via their cell phone]. It's very intoxicating."[40]

Sitting in a restaurant and just eating a meal is difficult for many people. Even when they are eating with friends, people often pull out their phones to check messages, news updates, or social media sites.

Robert Piper, a blogger for the *Huffington Post*, also points out that cell phones have the potential to drive people apart:

> How many relationships are lost because of lack of [face-to-face] communication? Think about what a parent is doing to a child's emotional well-being when they're focused on their cell phone rather than their children. . . . Everything in this world is instant gratification—we focus on how many likes we get on our Facebook post, how many retweets on our Twitter page.[41]

Obsessive Checking

Piper reports that according to a 2013 report on Internet trends, the average American checks his or her smartphone 150 times a day. Other studies have shown that people cannot set aside their phones even at night. According to the *Time* Mobility Poll, a 2012 survey of cell phone users in eight countries (the United States, Great Britain, South Korea, China, India, South Africa, Indonesia, and Brazil), 50 percent of Americans sleep with their phone next to them in bed. Considering this habit by age group, 75 percent of twenty-five- to twenty-nine-year-olds sleep with their phones, and more than 80 percent of eighteen- to twenty-four-year-olds do so. Moreover, among all the countries surveyed, 84 percent of cell phone users said they could not go a single day without their phones. Twenty-five percent check their phone every thirty minutes, and 20 percent check it every ten minutes.

"People have no tolerance for boredom. They can't tolerate not doing something, because they have the world in their pockets [via their cell phone]."[40]

—*Psychiatrist David Greenfield.*

Given such excessive behavior, many people view cell phone use as more than just a habit. Film reviewer Stephen Whitty states, "It is an addiction, except no one wants to kick it." He adds that this addiction keeps cell phone users from participating in the world around them:

> People stumble blindly up stairs and down sidewalks because they can't bear to look away from their self-reflecting, self-promoting toys. You think they're going to put them away just because they're sitting next to strangers in a darkened theater?

You think they're going to stop writing about themselves just so they can listen to someone else? And so they sit there, texting "LOL!" instead of actually laughing, messaging "friends" instead of actually being with some.[42]

Phones as an Extension of Self

Indeed, even some cell phone users admit that their devices are keeping them from doing other things, and studies have found that many of them consider themselves addicted to their phones. One such study, conducted in 2010 by the International Center for the Media & the Public Agenda of the University of Maryland, involved college students from twelve universities on five different continents (Asia, Africa, Europe, North America, and South America). Participants were asked to abstain from using various forms of media—e-mail, Facebook, mobile phones, texting, music, news, and television—for twenty-four hours, after which they reported how they felt during this period. The students' reactions were then analyzed by category: media type, emotional type, and country.

In reporting the overall results of the study on the blog *The World Unplugged*, researchers stated that "students reported that media—especially their mobile phones—have literally become an extension of themselves. Going without media, therefore, made it seem like they had lost part of themselves."[43] Other researchers have also noted that people can sometimes become emotionally attached to their cell phones. Researchers at the Queensland University of Technology in Australia, for example, conducted surveys in 2011 that showed that many teens and young adults view their cell phones as part of themselves.

Psychologist Ira Hyman discusses this work:

Identifying your cell phone as part of your self predicts not simply how frequently people use their phones, but also their involvement with their phones. Mobile phone involvement included measures such as keeping your phone nearby, thinking frequently about your phone, interrupting activities to respond to your phone, feeling distressed without your phone, and being unable to reduce phone use.[44]

A Form of Abuse

Although cell phones can be valuable tools of communication, they can also be used to hurt, control, harass, intimidate, humiliate, or obsessively keep tabs on another person. Incidents where texting is used for this purpose are on the rise. Experts call this *textual harassment.* Addressing this problem in regard to teen dating violence, the Indiana Coalition Against Domestic Violence asks, "Are frequent texts just chatting and checking in, or are they an attempt to control? Constant texts asking where you are, who you are with, what you are doing, what you are wearing, etc., are designed to limit social interactions and friendships outside of the dating relationship." Experts say that such behavior is becoming more common, especially among teens. Half of the fourteen- to twenty-four-year-olds responding to a recent Associated Press/MTV Survey said that they had experienced some form of digital abuse, including textual harassment, from a dating partner, a friend, or a bullying schoolmate.

Indiana Coalition Against Domestic Violence, "Teen Dating Violence Facts." www.icadvinc.org.

Nomophobia

Sometimes this distress over not having a phone can develop into a phobia—a fear of being without a mobile phone or out of mobile phone contact (such as occurs when a phone runs out of batteries or a phone user cannot get a signal). The term for this, which was coined by British researchers in 2008, is *nomophobia* (for "no-mobile-phone phobia"). Between then and 2012, when the phobia was studied by mobile technology security company SecurEnvoy, the percentage of people who have this fear has risen from 53 percent to 66 percent. Similarly, a study conducted by Lookout, a smartphone security company, found that 73 percent of Americans go into a panic when they cannot find their phone.

Few studies have been done on nomophobia, and of these the number of people being studied has been small. One study from the MGM Medical College in India, for example, examined only two hundred college students. Nonetheless, the authors of the 2010 study were able to conclude that one in five college students in India are no-mophobic. (After China, India is the largest mobile phone market in the world, with nearly 885 million mobile connections as of the end of 2012.) The researchers also warned that the number of nomophobia sufferers is likely to rise to epidemic proportions, not just in India but elsewhere, as millions of people in countries around the world join the ranks of cell phone users every month.

Anxiety and Depression

In the World Unplugged study, participants also talked of experiencing an anxiety over their lack of phone access that suggested nomophobia. For example, a student from China reported, "I would feel irritable, tense, restless and anxious when I could not use my mobile phone. When I couldn't communicate with my friends, I felt so lonely, as if I was in a small cage in a solitary island." Another student, this one from Mexico, said,

> I felt curious and impotent because I could not use [my phone] even for a few minutes to check if there was some important message. I went to have lunch with my family and in order to avoid temptation, I left my phone at home. It is noteworthy that during the meal, as I was seeing most of the people there using their cell phones, I began to feel stress and despair for having left mine for the first time and on purpose.[45]

In addition, the World Unplugged researchers noted that many of the participants were substituting virtual relationships for real ones, which for some meant that they felt as close to their media as they would to a friend. Wrote a student from Chile: "I felt lonely without multimedia. I arrived at the conclusion that media is a great companion."[46]

A study conducted by researchers at Kent State University in 2013 also found that college students who use their phones heavily experience negative emotions, like anxiety and loneliness. In addition, it found that these individuals are less satisfied with their lives and get lower grades than students who are far less dependent on their phones. Moreover, psychiatrists note that when patients who are heavy cell phone users come to them with such problems, they often use their phones as a way to avoid facing difficult issues. As Victor Fornari, director of the division of child and adolescent psychiatry at North Shore–LIJ Health System in New Hyde Park, New York, reports, "I have kids come to my office for treatment, and if their phone goes off, they take the call, or if they don't like what we're talking about, they pull out their phone and start playing a video game."[47]

> "I would feel irritable, tense, restless and anxious when I could not use my mobile phone. When I couldn't communicate with my friends, I felt so lonely, as if I was in a small cage in a solitary island."[45]
>
> —A student from China.

Sleep Problems

Experts note that cell phones can also cause sleep problems, which in turn can produce anxiety and stress. Dr. David Connington of the Melbourne Sleep Disorder Center explains that people who have difficulty disconnecting from their daily lives and from all of the information that cell phones provide can experience problems when they try to fall asleep. He explains, "People are doing so much during a normal day that it can mean that they feel like they're 'on call' even at night. Because it's so easy to receive emails constantly, and get notifications from smartphones, it becomes more difficult for us to separate our waking and sleeping lives."[48]

Mental health can be affected when receiving and sending texts keeps people from getting a good night's sleep. As Texas pediatrician Ari Brown reports,

> Teenagers probably get the least sleep out of many age groups, and they really need that sleep because they're still growing, and their brains are growing, and they're super busy during the day. If you are already getting a limited number of hours of sleep, and then the quality is worsened—even if you don't remember it—that's a cause for concern.[49]

Perhaps even more concerning is that some people cannot help texting in their sleep. Michael Breus, a clinical psychologist and sleep specialist, explains, "It's basically what we call an arousal disorder. Somebody gets woken up [by an outside stimulus] but is not completely awake from the process of sleeping. People will reach over, and not even half awake, will start answering their texts."[50] Sometimes the sleep-texting person texts gibberish, other times the sent messages make sense, but in either case the person typically does not remember the experience upon waking.

The Ability to Wait

Such behavior has led many people to consider cell phone use an addiction. In fact, in the World Unplugged study, participants repeatedly spoke of being addicted to media in general, and particularly to their mobile phones. In addition, the language they used in talking about how they felt without access to their addiction was similar to what drug addicts feel when they are going through withdrawal. For example, one student from the United States said, "I was itching, like a crackhead, because I could not use my phone."[51] Given that so many students in the study used this kind of language, the researchers concluded that "students' 'addiction' to media may not be clinically diagnosed, but the cravings sure seem real—as does the anxiety and the depression."[52]

Since anxiety, depression, and the inability to face up to problems are often associated with addictions to drugs and alcohol, some people take this as evidence that cell phones are addictive in the same sense as these substances. To test the addictive nature of cell phones, Paul Atchley, a professor of psychology at the University of Kansas, devised a study to determine whether cell phones are truly an addiction for people who seem addicted to them. Assisted by one of his undergraduate students, Amelia Warden, he gave one hundred college students a choice between receiving a small amount of money to respond to a text immediately or a larger amount of money if they delayed responding to the text.

Atchley explains the reasoning behind his study: "If you think about being addicted to something, you're not really willing to wait to engage in that behavior. If you're addicted to alcohol, you'd rather have one beer now than two cases of beer in a week. So we simply did

Too little sleep can harm a person's health. Yet many teenagers, and some adults, cannot resist checking their phones during the night when they are supposed to be sleeping.

that within the context of texting to see what the decision-making profile looked like."[53]

The researchers discovered that unlike people who are addicted to substances like alcohol, cell phone users do have some self-control when it comes to their desire to text—but not much. According to Atchley and Warden,

What we found is, people are willing to wait, but they aren't willing to wait that long. I think this is because responding to a text doesn't make sense if too much time goes by. If you asked me a question and it takes me a day to get the answer to you, there's probably no purpose to me responding at that point. So, young adults feel like they need to respond quickly for it to be relevant.[54]

Atchley and Warden also tested whether the identity of the person sending a text would make a difference to test subjects, telling different subjects that different individuals were trying to communicate with them. Atchley reports, "If you're talking about texting an acquaintance back, people are willing to wait almost indefinitely to get that monetary reward. But if it's someone closer to them, that changes. People were willing to give us $25 back, to have the opportunity to text their girlfriend or boyfriend back within 20 minutes."[55]

But because test subjects were willing to wait under certain circumstances, the researchers concluded that they were not operating under an addiction but rather a compulsion—an urge that is not as irresistible as an addiction but nearly so. Hyman agrees with this conclusion. He says, "I'm not sure we want to call this an addiction yet. Instead, I think we are seeing an emerging form of social interaction."[56]

> "Cell phones are a part of our consumer culture. They are not just a consumer tool, but are used as a status symbol."[58]
>
> —*James Roberts, a professor of marketing at Baylor University's Hankamer School of Business.*

A Better Life

For some people this form of interaction has positive social and psychological effects. This is particularly the case, according to the *Time* Mobility Poll, for people who are highly educated and make a medium to high income (called *elites* by the poll). As Gibbs reports:

Elites are more likely to say that they work longer hours and have less time to think but also that [mobility] has made them more efficient and productive, able to manage more, be away

Sexting

In October 2013 approximately thirty teens in San Diego, California, were involved in a sexting scandal that might lead to felony charges against some of them. Sexting is the texting of a nude, partially nude, or otherwise sexually suggestive photo or video, and sending such images over the Internet is illegal. In this case about a dozen of the teens used their cell phones to take photos of themselves and text them to their boyfriends. They never dreamed that the photos would end up being shared via the Internet with students at seven different schools—which is exactly what happened.

Surveys have shown that more than 70 percent of girls who have sexted intended their photos to be for their boyfriends alone, and roughly 70 percent of boys who have sexted say their images were for girlfriends. But as with the San Diego teens, these photos often end up in other hands. Sometimes this is because the recipient wants to share the images with friends, perhaps as a way to brag about a sexual conquest. In other cases the recipient is engaging in what experts call revenge porn, whereby someone who has been dumped by a boyfriend or girlfriend shares previously received images as a way to exact revenge on the person who dumped him or her.

from the office, stay informed about the news and be a better parent. Four in 10 Americans think mobility has helped them achieve a better work-life balance, vs. three-quarters or more of Indians, Indonesians, Chinese and South Africans.[57]

Given the feelings of the elites, it is not surprising that researchers found that some people view a cell phone as a symbol of wealth and prestige. James Roberts, a professor of marketing at Baylor University's Hankamer School of Business, says, "Cell phones are a part of our consumer culture. They are not just a consumer tool, but are used as a status symbol."[58] In conducting a study into heavy cell phone use among college students, Roberts found that many young people felt that losing their cell phone would negatively impact their social lives.

Roberts believes that such attitudes are unhealthy. However, he acknowledges that it is unlikely that people will become any less dependent on their phones, especially since surveys indicate that 90 percent of college students use their cell phones daily and that the average college student spends seven hours a day interacting with communication technology. Many other experts agree with this assessment. They also note that even people whose phone use is taking a toll on their personal relationships are often loathe to leave their phones turned off, even for just a little while.

A Hidden Threat?

O n July 31, 2013, NASA released a report from its Aviation Safety Reporting System (ASRS) that provided examples of recent trouble reports on aircraft involving passengers' electronic devices. Some of these involved a device catching on fire, typically because of a damaged battery. Others involved passengers arguing with flight attendants or other passengers because of inconsiderate or disallowed device use. But a few of the reports told of devices that seemed to adversely affect pilots' instruments.

For example, one report noted, "First Officer reports compass system malfunctions during initial climb. When passengers are asked to verify that all electronic devices are turned off the compass system returns to normal." Another stated that a "portable Garmin GPS [global positioning system device] . . . allegedly interfered with a . . . navigation update function." Still another reported that the "fuel gauge blanked after [takeoff] and became operable prior to [landing]. Crew suspects possible [personal electronic device] interference."[59]

This was not the first time that an airplane crew had suspected that personal electronic devices, including cell phones, were causing problems with their instruments. Since 2000, pilots have filed at least ten reports with the ASRS claiming that electronic interference was to blame for an instrument not working properly. Moreover, in 2011 a report by the International Air Transport Association (IATA) revealed that seventy-five incidents had occurred between 2003 and 2009 in which personal electronic devices appeared to have caused problems related to aircraft instrumentation. Twenty-nine of them involved cell phones. These incidents took place on 125 different airlines, and the effects seen included the malfunctioning of GPS receivers and altitude control readings, the failure of landing gear to drop into position, and the disengagement of an autopilot device.

Dave Carson of the aircraft company Boeing, who studied this issue as part of a US advisory group, says that the navigational system malfunctions could be considered serious if they occurred when it came time to land the plane. As he explains, "It could be that you were to the right of the runway when in fact, you were to the left of the runway, or just completely wipe out the signal so that you didn't get any indication of where you are coming in."[60]

Another Boeing expert, engineer Kenny Kirchoff, points out that just the distraction of a malfunctioning instrument could be dangerous, especially when the pilot is trying to land the plane. "It's not necessarily that a phone can bring down an airplane," he states. "That's not really the issue. The issue is interfering with the airplane and causing more work for the pilots during critical phases of flight. So when they take off and when they land, those are phases of flight which require a high level of concentration by the pilots."[61] If a pilot's attention is compromised at such a time, an accident could occur and people could be hurt or killed.

A Possibility

In all of the IATA cases, once passengers were admonished to check their personal devices and turn them off if they had not already done so, the airplane's instruments began working normally again.

Consequently, the pilots and crew members involved in the incidents were convinced that the devices were to blame. According to CNN reporters Mike M. Ahlers and Rene Marsh, because these individuals are credible sources, "those who flatly say there's no evidence that electronic devices have caused interference on planes are wrong."[62]

In 2013 the Federal Aviation Administration (FAA) stated that studies on the use of portable electronic devices on airplanes are being conducted to see whether such devices can indeed cause problems with aircraft instrumentation. In the meantime, such devices must be turned off during takeoffs and landings when the

> "Those who flatly say there's no evidence that electronic devices have caused interference on planes are wrong."[62]
>
> —CNN reporters Mike M. Ahlers and Rene Marsh.

Personal electronic devices, including cell phones, are a concern on airplanes. Some experts say that these devices can interfere with aircraft instruments but research into this issue is ongoing.

plane is at an altitude of 10,000 feet (3,048 m) or lower. In a 2013 fact sheet on its website, the agency explains the rationale behind this rule:

> The technology for portable electronic devices (PEDs) has been around for many years and is still used in today's electronics, but there are many uncertainties about the radio signals the devices give off. Even PEDs that do not intentionally transmit signals can emit unintentional radio energy. This energy may affect aircraft safety because the signals can occur at the same frequencies used by the plane's highly sensitive communications, navigation, flight control and electronic equipment.

Current FAA guidance says passengers should turn off tablets, e-readers and any other PEDs with an "OFF" switch during takeoff and landing. This is to prevent potential interference that could pose a safety hazard as the cockpit crew focuses on arrival and departure duties. On a given flight, there could be hundreds of different PEDs in many different states of function or repair giving off spurious signals, so without proper testing there is no assurance they will not produce interference during these critical phases of flight.[63]

The FAA also says, "Cell phones (and other intentional transmitters) differ from most PEDs in that they are designed to send out signals strong enough to be received at great distances."[64] Because of this, in 1991 the Federal Communications Commission (FCC) banned the in-flight use of cell phones because it could interfere with cell phone networks on the ground as the planes passed over them.

"We can't say categorically that these devices cause interference."[65]

—IATA spokesman Chris Goater.

Today, however, smartphones have an airplane mode that disables the transmitter and allows the phone to access the cellular data network. Consequently, airlines now allow passengers to have their phones on during a flight as long as they are in airplane mode, which means the user cannot make calls, send texts, or access the Internet but can still access content already stored in the phone, such as notes and games.

Unnecessary Precautions

In setting such restrictions, the FAA emphasizes that its goal is public safety. It is unwilling to risk people's health for the sake of a cell phone call. Some people, however, believe that these restrictions are unnecessary. They point out that no scientific studies have proved that cell phones and other personal electronic devices can cause any problems to aircraft instrumentation. In fact, in tests conducted by American Airlines, phone calls made from various kinds of airplanes parked with their

Airline Controversy

In December 2013 the FCC was considering whether to allow cell phone use during US flights. The agency's leaders expected the public to express some concerns about safety issues in regard to this decision, but they did not expect the outcry over what the chairman of the FCC, Tom Wheeler, called "the consternation caused by the thought of your onboard seatmate disturbing the flight making phone calls." Wheeler acknowledged that he understood such concerns but did not feel he should have to take possible rudeness into account when making his decision. He said, "I do not want the person in the seat next to me yapping at 35,000 feet [10,668 m] any more than anyone else. But we are not the Federal Courtesy Commission." He said that his focus was solely on the technology, explaining, "Technology has produced a new network reality [picocell] recognized by governments and airlines around the world. Our responsibility is to recognize that new reality's impact on our old rules."

Quoted in Cecilia Kang, "Controversy over Proposal to Allow Cellphone Calls in Flight Tests New FCC Chairman Wheeler," *Washington Post*, December 12, 2013. www.washingtonpost.com.

instrumentation on at various airports did not have any effect on any aircraft instruments. IATA spokesman Chris Goater says, "We can't say categorically that these devices cause interference."[65]

Goater adds, though, that the pilots' reports should give people pause. Some frequent flyers disagree. For example, Phil Walsh, a businessman from Mobile, Alabama, says, "I have been flying for more than a decade. I have always sneaked and used my cell phone and laptop. Never heard of any problems and landed safely every time."[66]

Kyle Vanhemert, who writes for the technology website Gizmodo, is more emphatic in his rejection of cell phone concerns. He states, "The thing about the electromagnetic interference is that it's a lie." He believes that the FAA and the FCC banned in-flight cell phone use not because they had proof that cell phones were a problem but because "it seemed feasible that they *could*" cause a problem. Vanhemert sarcastically adds, "Sure, cell phones *might* cause interference. But a megashark *might* jump out of the water and bite your plane in half, too."[67]

No Proof

Even Ahlers and Marsh admit that there is no proof that using a cell phone during a flight has caused a plane to crash. They say, "We can find no instance in which electromagnetic interference from a portable electronic device brought down a commercial plane or was a contributing factor in an accident. And the National Transportation Safety Board says it has never issued a recommendation [a safety warning] about such devices on planes."[68]

> "Sure, cell phones *might* cause interference. But a megashark *might* jump out of the water and bite your plane in half, too."[67]
>
> —Kyle Vanhemert of the technology website Gizmodo.

However, the circumstances surrounding some crashes have made a few safety experts suspect that cell phone–related instrument interference might have played a role in the crash. Among the most notable was the crash of a charter flight in 2003 in Christchurch, New Zealand, that killed eight people. The pilot, who was talking on his cell phone, mistimed his landing so that he struck the ground shortly before reaching the runway. Some say the distraction of the call was what caused him to crash, much the way texting while driving can cause a car crash. But in its final report on the plane crash, the New Zealand Transport Accident Investigation Commission stated that the pilot's cell phone might have caused a navigational aid to give a false reading.

Newer Airplanes

Some people say that although it is possible that cell phones might have played a role in navigational problems in the past, modern planes are very unlikely to be affected by them. This is because they are now being built with features that make it harder for electromagnetic interference to reach instrumentation. But experts worry that such improvements might not be keeping pace with advancing portable electronic-device technology. As Doug Hughes, an electrical engineer and air safety investigator, explains, "The technical advancements for wireless devices and portable electronic equipment is so rapid, it changes every week. The advances in airplanes take 20 years."[69]

Moreover, some airlines are unwilling to pay for more advanced technologies. Chris Cooke, writing for *Executive Travel* magazine, explains: "Avionics systems have expanded and improved as well, but many airlines haven't committed the resources to upgrading to the more advanced units. As a result, some aircraft are still equipped with older electronics that are more susceptible to radio frequency interference."[70]

Engineer Bill Strauss, an expert in issues related to the use of personal electronic devices on airplanes, says there is another factor to consider: the fact that aging airplanes and devices do not always perform the way they did when they were new. According to Strauss,

> A plane is designed to the right specs, but nobody goes back and checks if it is still robust. Then there are the outliers—a cellphone that's been dropped and abused, or a battery that puts out more than it's supposed to, and avionics that are more susceptible to interference because gaskets have failed. And boom, that's where you get interference. It would be a perfect storm that would combine to create an aviation accident.[71]

Output Power

Despite such concerns, some countries allow the use of cell phones on their airlines, and this apparently has not caused any ill effects. Vanhemert takes this as proof that worries about cell phones on American planes are overblown. Experts, however, point out that in many cases the planes allowing the use of cell phones are equipped with new technology that changes the way the cell phone signals are transmitted.

Specifically, the airplanes have a picocell, a low-power base station that essentially creates a network area encompassing the cabin of the plane and all the phones being used within it. This base station routes phone traffic to a communications satellite in orbit around Earth. The satellite then transmits this traffic to a base station on the ground, and from there it goes to a cell network. In explaining this device, technology writer Meghan Neal says, "If you stick one on an airplane, you've got a micro, mobile cellular network in the sky. . . . [But] the equipment is rigged to control the transmission so it doesn't try to directly contact cell networks on the ground, which would interfere with those signals."[72]

Neal goes on to explain how this protects the instrumentation on board the aircraft: "Basically, since the antenna on the picocell is so close to the phones onboard that it's communicating with, the output power can be very low. FAA restrictions mandate that cell signals are at their lowest transmitting power level, minimizing the risk that the transmission will get all tangled up in the aircraft equipment signals."[73] (Aircraft wi-fi services, which allow passengers to access the Internet using a laptop, rely on a dedicated air-to-ground frequency that does not pose an interference risk.)

Medical Devices

Experts say that other types of equipment, including medical devices, can also be affected by cell phone transmissions. When a cell phone is used very close to these devices, it is possible that the phone will interfere with their operation and threaten someone's health. Julia Marders and Donald Witters of the Center for Devices and Radiological Health explain in an article shared on the US Food and Drug Administration (FDA) website:

> Under certain conditions, cell phone radio transmissions can cause electromagnetic interference (EMI) and disrupt the function of electrically powered medical devices. . . . Although EMI-related patient injuries are relatively rare, sources of electromagnetic energy such as radio signals, AC power line

Medical Apps

Although some medical professionals are concerned about the use of smartphones around medical equipment, others see the advantages that this technology has for the medical field. Specifically, they are excited about applications, or apps, that can turn smartphones into medical devices, such as heart monitors, blood pressure gauges, ophthalmoscopes (to check eyes for glaucoma), and dermatoscopes (which can check skin for symptoms of cancer). In speaking about these apps, Dr. Jeffrey Shuren, director of the FDA's Center for Devices and Radiological Health, says, "Mobile apps have the potential to transform health care by allowing doctors to diagnose patients with potentially life-threatening conditions outside of traditional health care settings, help consumers manage their own health and wellness, and also gain access to useful information whenever and wherever they need it." In September 2013, the FDA announced that it will regulate these apps to ensure that they work properly and safely.

RT: Question More, "FDA Announces Regulation for Increasingly Popular Mobile Phone Medical Apps," September 24, 2013. http://rt.com.

disruptions, and electrostatic discharge can disrupt medical device performance.[74]

As an example, they report that on one occasion when the visitor of a patient in the intensive care unit received a phone call, the patient's infusion pump—which was delivering the drug epinephrine into the patient's body at a controlled rate—increased the rate at which the medication was being dripped. As a result, the patient received an overdose of the drug and became sicker.

Events like this occur because of the way cell phones operate. BBC health and technology reporter Claudia Hammond explains:

Whenever a phone is switched on it transmits a signal hoping to make contact with a base station in order to send and receive calls or texts and with smartphones, emails and other data. Once these electromagnetic waves are being transmitted, any length of wire in a piece of medical equipment can act as an antenna. In principle, even the wire linking a patient to a monitor could do it. It's the resulting electric current which could disrupt the equipment.[75]

An implantable defibrillator, or pacemaker, is visible in this color-enhanced X-ray of a patient's chest cavity. Medical devices such as this may be vulnerable to disruption by cell phones.

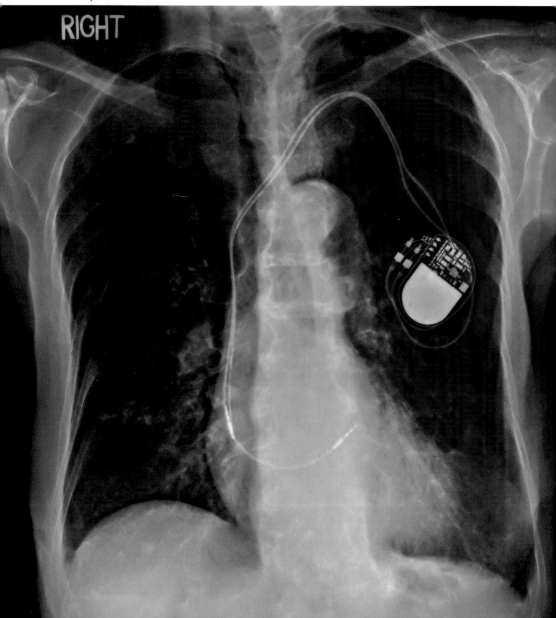

Hammond adds that a phone's ability to interfere with devices is affected by the intensity of its signal, the signal's frequency, and the effectiveness of the shielding built into the equipment. This explains why a study conducted by Dutch researchers found that when sixty-one medical devices used in critical care were subjected to cell phone transmissions, 43 percent of them were adversely affected. During testing of the medical devices, the phones were transmitting at their highest power (to simulate what happens when a cell phone is struggling to find a signal) and were extremely close to the devices being tested, most often only 1 inch (3 cm) away. This means that the devices were being subjected to an intense signal. Moreover, the study was conducted in 2009, when devices had less effective shielding and longer internal wires than they do today; these factors made it easier for the signal to reach the internal workings of the devices.

Have Deaths Occurred?

Stories abound on the Internet of deaths occurring due to cell phone interference with medical devices. However, the website Snopes, which investigates the validity of rumors, has declared that these stories are false, and there is no evidence to suggest otherwise. Nonetheless, Snopes cautions,

> Although no real deaths have yet occurred, enough scary incidents have been attributed to cell phones that at least some hospitals have banned the use of those devices on their premises, or at least in their trauma, critical care, and surgical areas. Cell phone interference has supposedly created false alarms in infant incubators, prompted heart monitors to spew false results (making it appear as if patients hooked up to them were in cardiac arrest), set off fire alarms, caused IV pumps to stop working, and contributed to failures in equipment necessary for the maintenance of life itself.[76]

As an example of the latter, Snopes reports that a breathing machine for infants at Baylor University Medical Center in Dallas,

Texas, stopped working when a staff member turned on a cell phone while this piece of equipment was being tested with no patient attached to it.

Restrictions on Use

Two other devices whose operation can be disrupted by cell phone use are pacemakers and implantable defibrillators, both used to keep the heart beating normally. The FDA reports that if electromagnetic interference were to affect such devices, it could cause them to work improperly or stop working altogether. However, the FDA notes that the manufacturers of these devices subject them to testing to ensure that they are safe from cell phone interference; thus, if the medical device is working properly, no problems should occur. Consequently, the FDA states that, "based on current research, cell phones would not seem to pose a significant health problem for the vast majority of pacemaker wearers."[77]

> "With the exception of holding phones next to critical care equipment, there is no convincing evidence supporting blanket bans on the grounds of electromagnetic interference."[79]
>
> —BBC reporter Claudia Hammond.

Yet according to the American Heart Association, new technology might increase the risk of cell phone interference with pacemakers. The organization explains that "technology is rapidly changing as the Federal Communications Commission (FCC) makes new frequencies available. Newer cellphones using these new frequencies might make pacemakers less reliable. A group of cellphone companies is studying that possibility."[78] Given this possibility, many experts recommend that people implanted with a pacemaker avoid carrying a turned-on cell phone in the chest pocket of a shirt or jacket as a precautionary measure. Experts recommend that a turned-on cell phone not be placed extremely close to other medical devices as well. In fact, some hospitals do not allow cell phones anywhere near critical pieces of equipment. Other hospitals do not restrict cell phone use in this way, believing it to be unnecessary.

Hammond agrees that it is unnecessary for hospitals to restrict cell phone use simply on the basis of how phones might affect medical devices. She states, "With the exception of holding phones next to critical care equipment, there is no convincing evidence supporting blanket bans on the grounds of electromagnetic interference."[79] Nonetheless, she points out another reason why hospitals might want to ban cell phones: phones are hard to wash and are therefore likely to harbor bacteria. Indeed, a study in India found that 95 percent of cell phones belonging to health care workers were contaminated with bacteria, and a similar study in Turkey found that 40 percent of hospital patients' phones were contaminated. Given such studies, it is far more likely that a person will become ill from using a cell phone than that an electronic device—medical, navigational, or otherwise—will stop working because of a phone call.

Introduction: Do Cell Phones Pose Risks to Human Health and Well-Being?

1. Quoted in *Northeast Times*, "Can You Imagine Life Without a Cell Phone?," June 19, 2013. www.northeasttimes.com.

2. Lee Rainie, "Cell Phone Ownership Hits 91% of Adults," Pew Research Center, June 6, 2013. www.pewresearch.org.

3. Daniel Cressey, "No Link Found Between Mobile Phones and Cancer," *Nature*, May 17, 2010. www.nature.com.

4. Mark Glaser, "How Cell Phones Are Killing Face-to-Face Interactions," PBS MediaShift, October 22, 2007. www.pbs.org.

Chapter One: Can Cell Phones Cause Cancer?

5. Quoted in Bellinda Kontominas, "Research Underlines Powerline Cancer Risk," *Sydney Morning Herald*, August 22, 2007. www.smh.com.au.

6. Quoted in Kontominas, "Research Underlines Powerline Cancer Risk."

7. American Cancer Society, "Cellular Phone Towers," www.cancer.org.

8. American Cancer Society, "Cellular Phone Towers."

9. Quoted in India Infoline News Service, "Professor Michael Repacholi Releases 'Mobile Phones and Public Health—Myths and Reality,'" December 3, 2013. www.indiainfoline.com.

10. Quoted in India Infoline News Service, "Professor Michael Repacholi Releases 'Mobile Phones and Public Health—Myths and Reality.'"

11. Karen N. Peart, "Cell Phone Use in Pregnancy May Cause Behavioral Disorders in Offspring," *Yale News*, March 15, 2012. http://news.yale.edu.

12. Quoted in Peart, "Cell Phone Use in Pregnancy May Cause Behavioral Disorders in Offspring."

13. Quoted in Emily, "Important New Russian Research on Cell Phone Radiation's Effect on Cognitive and Other Functions in Children," *Electromagnetic Health Blog*, April 11, 2011. http://electromagnetichealth.org.

14. Markham Heid, "Is Your Cell Phone Cooking Your Brain?," *Men's Health*, December 18, 2012. www.menshealth.com.

15. Quoted in *Talk of the Nation*, "Cell Phone Radiation Affects Brain, Study Says," NPR, February 25, 2011. www.npr.org.

16. Quoted in *Talk of the Nation*, "Cell Phone Radiation Affects Brain, Study Says."

17. Quoted in *Talk of the Nation*, "Cell Phone Radiation Affects Brain, Study Says."

18. Quoted in *Talk of the Nation*, "Cell Phone Radiation Affects Brain, Study Says."

19. Quoted in Heid, "Is Your Cell Phone Cooking Your Brain?"

20. Quoted in Cindy Stauffer, "Woman Wonders if Cellphone Stored in Bra Caused Her Breast Cancer," Lancaster Online, September 30, 2013. http://lancasteronline.com.

Chapter Two: The Hazards of Distraction

21. Quoted in Billy Hallowell, "Young Woman Could Spend 10 Years in Prison for Allegedly Killing Motorcyclist While Text Messaging," *Blaze*, October 9, 2013. www.theblaze.com.

22. Quoted in Michael Inbar, "Parents of Teen Who Died Texting and Driving: 'Kids Think They're Invincible,'" *Today Show*, March 5, 2012. www.today.com.

23. Quoted in Delthia Ricks, "Study: Texting While Driving Leading Cause of Death for Teen Drivers," *Newsday*, May 8, 2013. www.newsday.com.

24. Quoted in Kie Relyea, "Study: Texting While Driving Far More Common than Previously Thought," *Bellingham (WA) Herald*, September 10, 2013. www.bellinghamherald.com.

25. Quoted in Relyea, "Study."

26. Quoted in Jim Forsyth, "Texting While Driving More Dangerous than Thought," Reuters, October 5, 2011. www.reuters.com.

27. Texas A&M Transportation Institute, "New Study Says Texting Doubles a Driver's Reaction Time," October 5, 2001. http://tti.tamu.edu.

28. Michael Austin, "Texting While Driving: How Dangerous Is It?," *Car and Driver*, June 2009. www.caranddriver.com.

29. Phil LeBeau, "Texting and Driving Worse than Drinking and Driving," CNBC, June 25, 2009. www.cnbc.com.

30. Quoted in Associated Press, "California Cellphone Ban Reduces Traffic Related Deaths, Injuries, Berkeley Study Finds," *Huffington Post*, March 5, 2012. www.huffingtonpost.com.

31. Quoted in Adriana Lee, "Federal Survey: Laws Banning Cell Phone Use While Driving Aren't Working," TechnoBuffalo, April 9, 2013. www.technobuffalo.com.

32. Quoted in Dave Collins, "Conn. Teen Driver, Said to Be Using Cellphone, Is Charged in Jogger's Death," *Columbus (OH) Dispatch*, May 15, 2012. www.stamfordadvocate.com.

33. David L. Strayer and Frank A. Drews, "Cell-Phone–Induced Driver Distraction," *Current Directions in Psychological Science*, 2007, vol. 16, no. 3, p. 128. www.psych.utah.edu.

34. Quoted in Associated Press, "Distracted Driving Study: Cell Phone Dialing, Texting Dangerous. Talking? Less So," CBS News, January 2, 2014. www.cbsnews.com.

35. Quoted in Texas A&M Transportation Institute, "Voice-to-Text Apps Offer No Driving Safety Benefit; as with Texting, Reaction Times Double," press release, April 23, 2013. http://tti.tamu.edu.

Chapter Three: Threats to Social and Psychological Well-Being

36. Jeffrey Wells, "Stupid Tragedy, Yes, but Is Anyone Surprised?," Hollywood Elsewhere, January 13, 2014. www.hollywood-else where.com.

37. CBSNews.com Staff, "Cell Phones Ring Up Rage," CBS News, August 2, 2000. www.cbsnews.com.

38. Joan Johnson-Freese, "Cell Phone Rage," *It's Not Me, Right?* (blog), Barrington Patch, October 24, 2013. http://barrington .patch.com.

39. Nancy Gibbs, "Your Life Is Fully Mobile," *Time,* Mobile Tech Special, August 16, 2012. http://techland.time.com.

40. Quoted in MSN Money Partner, "5 Ways to Kick Your Tech Addiction in 2014," TechBiz, December 19, 2013. http://money .msn.com.

41. Robert Piper, "Your Cell Phone Is Not Your Body—You Can Let It Go," *Huffington Post,* September 24, 2013. www.huffington post.com.

42. Stephen Whitty, "Cell Phones in Movie Theaters, and Other Hangups," *New Jersey Star-Ledger,* October 17, 2013. www .nj.com.

43. *The World Unplugged* (blog), "Going 24 Hours Without Media." http://theworldunplugged.wordpress.com.

44. Ira Hyman, "Are You Addicted to Your Cell Phone?," *Mental Mishaps* (blog), Psychology Today, March 27, 2013. www.psycholo gytoday.com.

45. Quoted in *The World Unplugged* (blog), "Mobile Phones," http:// theworldunplugged.wordpress.com.

46. Quoted in *The World Unplugged* (blog), "Going 24 Hours Without Media."

47. Quoted in Barbara Bronson Gray, "Avid Cellphone Use by College Kids Tied to Anxiety, Lower Grades," HealthDay, December 12, 2013. http://consumer.healthday.com.

48. Quoted in Katherine Bindley, "Sleep Texting Is on the Rise, Experts Suggest," *Huffington Post*, February 14, 2013. www.huffingtonpost.com.

49. Quoted in Bindley, "Sleep Texting Is on the Rise, Experts Suggest."

50. Quoted in Bindley, "Sleep Texting Is on the Rise, Experts Suggest."

51. Quoted in *The World Unplugged* (blog), "Mobile Phones."

52. *The World Unplugged* (blog), "Going 24 Hours Without Media."

53. Quoted in KU News, "Research Shows Texting Is a Compulsion for Young Adults, if Not Quite an Addiction," University of Kansas, November 13, 2012. http://archive.news.ku.edu.

54. Quoted in Nikki Wentling, "University Research Shows Texting Is Compulsion for Young Adults," *University Daily Kansan*, University of Kansas–Lawrence, November 20, 2012. http://kansan.com.

55. Quoted in KU News, "Research Shows Texting Is a Compulsion for Young Adults, if Not Quite an Addiction."

56. Hyman, "Are You Addicted to Your Cell Phone?"

57. Gibbs, "Your Life Is Fully Mobile."

58. Quoted in Rick Nauert, "Compulsive Cell Phone Use Similar to Other Consumer 'Addictions,'" PsychCentral, November 29, 2012. http://psychcentral.com.

Chapter Four: A Hidden Threat?

59. NASA Aviation Safety Reporting System, "ASRS Database Report Set: Passenger Electronic Devices," July 31, 2013. http://asrs.arc.nasa.gov.

60. Quoted in Daniel Bates, "How Just One Mobile Phone Can Make a Plane Crash, Leaked Study Reveals," *Daily Mail* (London), June 10, 2011. www.dailymail.co.uk.

61. Quoted in Mike M. Ahlers and Rene Marsh, "Can Your Cell Phone Bring Down a Plane?," CNN, September 23, 2013. www.cnn.com.

62. Ahlers and Marsh, "Can Your Cell Phone Bring Down a Plane?"

63. Federal Aviation Administration, "Portable Electronic Devices," June 21, 2013. www.faa.gov.

64. Federal Aviation Administration, "Portable Electronic Devices."

65. Quoted in R. Leigh Coleman, "Can Cell Phones Cause Airplanes to Crash?," *Christian Post*, June 10, 2011. http://m.christianpost.com.

66. Quoted in Coleman, "Can Cell Phones Cause Airplanes to Crash?"

67. Kyle Vanhemert, "Cell Phones Don't Crash Airplanes," Gizmodo, February 3, 2011. http://gizmodo.com.

68. Ahlers and Marsh, "Can Your Cell Phone Bring Down a Plane?"

69. Quoted in Christine Negroni, "Interfering with Flight?," *New York Times*, January 17, 2011. www.nytimes.com.

70. Chris Cooke, "Understanding the In-Flight Cell Phone Ban," *Executive Travel*, September 2009. www.executivetravelmagazine.com.

71. Quoted in Negroni, "Interfering with Flight?"

72. Meghan Neal, "Mile Hi: Why It's Suddenly Safe to Use Cell Phones on Planes," *Motherboard* (blog), December 2013. http://motherboard.vice.com.

73. Neal, "Mile Hi."

74. Julia Marders and Donald Witters, "Don't Answer That Cell Phone," US Food and Drug Administration, March 21, 2013. www.fda.gov.

75. Claudia Hammond, "Are Mobile Phones Dangerous in Hospitals?," BBC, May 14, 2013. www.bbc.com.

76. Snopes, "Sick Call," August 16, 2008. www.snopes.com.

77. US Food and Drug Administration, "Radiation-Emitting Products." www.fda.gov.

78. American Heart Association, "Devices That May Interfere with Pacemakers," August 16, 2012. www.heart.org.

79. Hammond, "Are Mobile Phones Dangerous in Hospitals?"

Cell Phone Safety

website: cellphonesafety.org

Cell Phone Safety was created by the National Consumer Advocacy Commission, which works to educate consumers on safety and economic issues surrounding certain products and services. This website concentrates on issues related to the safety and financial concerns of cell phone use, including health hazards and how cell phones impact vehicular safety.

CTIA—the Wireless Association

1400 Sixteenth St., NW, Suite 600
Washington, DC 20036
phone: (202) 736-3200
website: www.ctia.org

Founded in 1984, this international nonprofit membership organization supports the wireless communications industry and provides information on cell phone–related issues, policies, and laws. It also promotes campaigns to educate the public on safe cell phone use.

Distracted Driving Foundation

13434 SE Twenty-Seventh Pl.
Bellevue, WA 98005
phone: (206) 919-1798
website: www.ddfn.org
e-mail: info@ddfn.org

This group works with technology providers, mobile carriers, and handset manufacturers to solve the problem of distracted driving as it relates to talking and texting on cell phones.

Federal Aviation Administration

800 Independence Ave. SW
Washington, DC 20591
phone: (866) TELL-FAA
website: www.faa.gov

This government agency is dedicated to providing the American public with the safest aerospace system in the world. Its website includes information on safety studies related to air travel and provides accident statistics.

National Cancer Institute

BG 9609 MSC 9760
9609 Medical Center Dr.
Bethesda, MD 20892-9760
phone: (800) 422-6237
website: www.cancer.gov

Part of the National Institutes of Health, this agency conducts and supports cancer research and provides information to the public on all types of cancer and cancer-related issues, including those connected to cell phone use.

Pew Research Center

1615 L St. NW, Suite 700
Washington, DC 20036
phone: (202) 419-4300
website: www.pewresearch.org
e-mail: info@pewresearch.org

The Pew Research Center is a nonpartisan research organization that provides information on a variety of issues, attitudes, and trends. Its Pew Internet & American Life Project specifically addresses the impact of the Internet on American life and society and has conducted studies related to cell phone use.

Text Free Driving Organization

website: www.textfreedriving.org

Based in Florida, this group is dedicated to raising awareness of the dangers of texting and working to support laws that would eliminate cell phone use while driving.

Texting Organization Against Distracted Driving, Inc.

531 Forest Oak Dr.
Stockbridge, GA 30281
phone: (678) 428-0046
website: www.toadd.org

Since October 2010 this organization has been dedicated to improving safety related to mobile phone technology by addressing the issues of distracted driving as well as sexting and cyberbullying.

US Food and Drug Administration

10903 New Hampshire Ave.
Silver Spring, MD 20993
phone: (888) 463-6332
website: www.fda.gov

This government agency is charged with protecting the health of the American public. To this end, it works to make sure that various drugs, products, and devices are safe. Its website provides articles regarding the impact of cell phone radiation emissions on human health and how these emissions affect medical devices.

World Health Organization (WHO)

Avenue Appia 20
1211 Geneva 27
Switzerland
phone: +41 22 791 21 11
website: www.who.int

A part of the United Nations system, this organization works globally to improve human health and supports research on a variety of health issues, including those related to cell phone use and electromagnetic and radiation emissions.

Books

Devra Davis, *Disconnect: The Truth About Cell Phone Radiation, What the Industry Is Doing to Hide It, and How to Protect Your Family*. New York: Dutton, 2010.

Cynthia Kempson and Eugene Rahm, eds., *Cell Phone Use and Health Risks: Assessments and State of Research*. Hauppauge, NY: Nova Science, 2013.

Stefan Kiesbye, *Cell Phones and Driving*. Farmington Hills, MI: Greenhaven, 2011.

Stefan Kiesbye, *Distracted Driving*. Farmington Hills, MI: Greenhaven, 2011.

Carla Mooney, *Thinking Critically: Cell Phones*. San Diego: ReferencePoint, 2014.

Alison Wilson, *Hold the Phone: The Definitive Guide to How to Protect Your Health from iPhones and Wireless*. Avonside, Australia: Avonside, 2013.

Internet Sources

American Cancer Society, "Cellular Phones." www.cancer.org/cancer/cancercauses/othercarcinogens/athome/cellular-phones.

Joanna Brenner, "Pew Internet: Mobile," PewResearch Internet Project, September 18, 2013. http://pewinternet.org/Commentary/2012/February/Pew-Internet-Mobile.aspx.

Edgar Snyder & Associates, "Cell Phone & Texting Accident Statistics." www.edgarsnyder.com/car-accident/cell-phone/cell-phone-statistics.html.

Jeffrey Kluger, "We Never Talk Any More: The Problem with Text Messaging," *Time*, September 6, 2012. www.cnn.com/2012/08/31/tech/mobile/problem-text-messaging-oms.

National Cancer Institute, "Cell Phones and Cancer Risk." www.cancer.gov/cancertopics/factsheet/Risk/cellphones.

Pew Research Center, "Teens and Distracted Driving," November 16, 2009. www.distraction.gov/download/research-pdf/PIP_Teens_and_Distracted_Driving.pdf.

Index

Picture Credits

Cover: Thinkstock Images

AP Images: 28

Apogee/Science Source: 58

© Jason Edwards/National Geographic Society/Corbis: 11

Mehau Kulyk/Science Photo Library: 17

© Matt Rourke/AP/Corbis: 32

Thinkstock Images: 7, 25, 38, 45

© DH Webster/Robert Harding World Imagery/Corbis: 51

About the Author

Patricia D. Netzley has written more than fifty books for children, teens, and adults. She has also worked as an editor, a writing instructor, and a knitting teacher. She is a member of the Society of Children's Book Writers and Illustrators.